life in tran
the journey that counts

Sam Berkson

> 'We conclusive proof of both the truth, the
> right Cause whether we hitchhike or push bike
> or travel kind of trash Manifest that.'

— Roots Manuva, *Witness (1 hope)*

Influx Press, London

Published by Influx Press
30 Northwold Road, London. N16 7EH
www.influxpress.com

First published 2012.

Printed and bound in the UK by the MPG Books Group,
Bodmin and King's Lynn.

ISBN 978-0-9571693-3-3

contents:

introduction

It is the journey that counts. A stock phrase, a cliché. Usually one of self-justification, consolation or commiseration. *Don't worry, mate, it's the journey that counts.* The destination has eluded us.

After 200,000 years of human existence we are still travellers unsure of our destination. The dream of the End of History, the great stop at the end of humanity's train journey where we can all finally collect our bags and walk off through the ticket barriers (should we be allowed a ticket that is) and into the land of plenty, has yet to happen, if it is to happen at all. Obversely, the narrative of continuous progress from the dark ages to the hi-tech, shining, scientific modern world of advanced thinking, tolerance and freedom, so much a part of our education programmes and public discourses, is patently, when looked at with even a moderately perceptive analysis, a mockery of a fiction. A fiction that mocks the lives of ninety per cent of the people on this planet.

So perhaps we are in the waiting room. A place cruelly named for its un-purpose. The only ends that we believe in now are apocalyptic. Climate-catastrophic, space-age disasters. A grandiose enlargement of our own personal disappearance into nothingness.

But as we are not looking forward (in either sense) to an end, it must be the journey that counts. In fact, there may be neither waiting nor arrival. Just a journey; the means that is the end.

This is not to suggest that we should all be 'living in the present' in nihilistic abandonment of all past and future, and that we should swap temporal consciousness for the immediate world of the senses. All living things have come from and are going somewhere. The future rushes on towards the present and then retreats away to the past.

Thus we make a life out of the transit. We know that how we travel and for what reasons are no more or less important than, and in fact directly related to, where we end up next.

But it is not a journey which we make alone. It is when our journeys collide with other journeyers (on public transport most often) that windows open into the lives of others, possibilities of what could be revealed by the occasion of what is. These transient meetings may show how diverse our routes are and how different our purposes, yet also they reveal how comprehensible they are to each other. It is the attempt to comprehend, to empathise and to understand that leads us to the necessary mutual aid and forgiveness (of self and others) that make the journey more worthwhile.

To understand and to forgive – tasks easier done sometimes in art than in life – as we continue ever in transit.

Sam Berkson - London, 2012

conversation

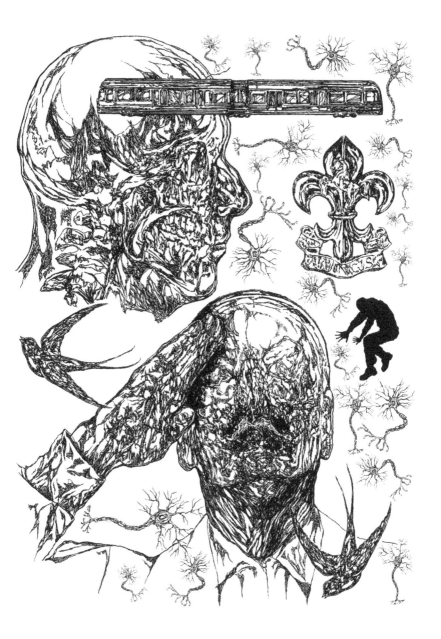

another veteran with a head wound

(London Paddington - Totnes; First Great Western)

> ***I see his uniform is woven / Of blood, bone, flesh and hair***
>
> – Adrian Mitchell

An ex-squaddie.
All misery and all lightness
council born and bred
scum of the earth, me.

Scum of the earth.
Not worth the lice his ma combed out of thick curls,
the 3rd of 5;
Not worth the flies that bothered his head,
now shaved,
in Kuwait;
and not worth much help after he'd served his time.

Now, he salutes me.

3791902 King's Regiment, Liverpool and Manchester.

On a mission to heal,

blood on his hands

and the death-mark of swallows

tattooed on his arms.

Came back from Kuwait in '91

stood by his mate through a brain tumour,

three years for stabbing someone.

Wife done the dirty behind his back

lost his house, lost his kids.

I'm all truth, me,

'cause it's in me, it's in you,

it's in all of us.

The voices talking through him as his voice talks through me.

5 years back,

he caught a man

earwigging

outside his house.

Smashed three panes of glass to get at him,

met the police when they came for him.

I'm anarchy, me.

I've done working, I've been there, believe me.

I'm English.

Proper English.

I'm a Celt.

C. E. L. T.

'Cause I'm English,

me ma's north Walian,

half me family's Irish

and me name's Scottish.

This is the longest I've had me hair,

rubbing his crewcut,

carrying the crosses of his nation

on a back that stood straight

for teachers, officers, wardens.

Half of what he says I don't understand
the other half I wish I didn't,
but he's talking to me.
I'm no wordsmith, he says,
but they – pointing at the football fans he's just been talking to
– They don't understand a fucking word.

The way it is,
the way he sees it,
it's not long before someone gets off their arse
and does something.

Came back from Kuwait in '91,
38 years a football fan,
built buildings enough,
all anarchy,
another veteran with a head wound.
I'm here to heal…
know yourself, son.

the inspector's discretion

(Liverpool Lime Street - London Euston; Virgin Trains)

'Yes sir, well it seems you only have
one outward bound ticket for these two journeys.
May I see the appropriate section
of this second ticket please?'

A young woman in her twenties,
all make-up and power dressing,
rummages for the missing ticket
and flips through reservations,
receipts and return tickets
inconclusively.
The man by her hurrying elbow
looks over her padded shoulder, vainly.

'Oh, I'm sure I picked it up,'
she says innocently.
'We have the receipt here', the man begins...
'I'm sure he understands, of course he does,'

her voice plummy and undaunted.
The man next to her is sleek and fat.
Maybe thirty years older than her, he bristles uncomfortably.

'Obviously we are trying to defraud you.'
Prickly humour. The brace buckles glint
at the waistband of his pin-striped trousers.

The ticket inspector is unmoved.
He looks down at them through fish bowl spectacles
and repeats in reedy, nasal tones,
'I'm going to have to sell you a full price single fare.'

The scene is set. The man is outraged.

'This is preposterous. Abso-bloody-lutely preposterous.
Of course we bought the ticket. Look, here's the receipt.'
Proof of his right hidden in the starred-out digits
of his platinum card.

The ticket inspector retains his calm,
'You may have bought a ticket, sir,
but how do I know that you haven't
given that ticket away to someone?'

'Do we look like the kind of people…'
his voice is rising, loud enough for all to hear.
Beginning to expose his hand
he lays out the cards
that this man cannot seem to read
through his thick-lensed spectacles.
'…The kind of people who would do a thing like that?' he asks.

'No,' I say, 'you don't look that generous,'
but only to myself.

We are nearing Milton Keynes and the scene ends.
Announcements to make,
the ticket inspector promises to return,
suggesting that they look again for the missing ticket.

Opposite the suspects, facing forward on the four-seater table

sits a thin, nervous looking woman

in a librarian's cardigan,

who has been bent over her book all this time,

sniffing apologetically.

Now she tries to help, offers them lines of defence.

From across the aisle, I do too.

Until now I have also kept my distance.

My ticket, as usual,

has had a previous stamp scrubbed off,

it only covers half my journey.

It wasn't that I forgot to buy the right one.

'These people don't know who they're talking to sometimes,'

he puffs.

'What if I tell him I've got colleagues at the bar?'

The girl giggles.

'It's an absolute disgrace hounding people like us,' he says.

'That man is a prat.'

The train pulls out of the station and
the ticket inspector returns.
'Now, have you found that ticket?'

The girl, keen to clear things up begins,
'I must have left it in the ticket machine or something
because it's just not in my handbag
but we really did buy two return tickets,
we've got all the other parts of it and the receipt.'

He has her now.
She has admitted her deed
(bulky ticket machine
hanging from his neck
in weighty authority),
this minor triumph will be his.
'I'm afraid that the rules state quite clearly
if you are travelling without the appropriate ticket...'

'This is too much,' the man snaps.

He jabs a sudden finger at this man in front of him

as he might swipe away a wasp with a copy of *The Telegraph*.

'You are a prat. An absolute prat.'

A challenge.

The inspector is lost for words.

'My PA here has three tickets and the receipt of purchase.

You know that we bought the ticket.

The actual presence of the fourth ticket is immaterial.

You know we haven't cheated anyone.'

'You have got on a train

without the correct ticket for the journey.

I am offering you the chance to buy a single ticket fare.'

Defensive jut of the chin,

holding the man's angry stare through his thick lenses.

'Do you have discretion

about whether or not you accept our explanation?'

our man (who has colleagues at the bar)

asks.

'If you are travelling without…' the inspector begins again.

'Answer the question,' the man interrupts,

triumphant now,

playing the Perry Mason,

the train carriage his audience and jury.

He sounds out his words loudly and slowly,

'Do you, or do you not, have discretion over the issuing of
fines?'

'Yes, I do,' he says.

'And so you can choose whether or not you issue a fine on this
occasion?'

'Yes sir, but I am choosing on this occasion to fine you

as I cannot be certain that you have not given the ticket

away to somebody else, thereby enabling

the evasion of a fare for this journey,'

says Mr Inspector Pratt.

'I'm going to announce the next station

and when I return I will ask again for the full single fare for
this journey.

If you don't pay I will call the transport police

and have them meet you at Euston station.'

The cornerstone threat of the interaction.

That quietens him a little.

The inspector leaves the carriage.

The man jumps out of his seat,
spreads his arms and addresses his audience.
'Who here thinks I should have to pay the fine?
You all heard him. What do you think?'
Smiling, jovial, intelligent.
'Should I have to pay the fine?'
The gentleman patrician appealing to his tenants.

And then you, from across the table,
quiet and awkward in your cardigan,
you, who would never cheat or buy the wrong ticket,
spoke up softly but firmly.
'I don't think it's very reasonable of him to ask you to pay,
but you didn't need to speak to him like that.'

Silence.

Mountains collapse

the sea rises up and swallows the land

cities crumble to dust

and forests spread across their ruined carcasses

birds drop dead out of the sky.

But only for a second.

'Well listen yes, I mean, absolutely,

I lost my temper and I shouldn't have spoken to him

in the way I did and you know

of course I can afford this ticket of course, yes.

Why weren't you paying attention at the ticket machine, Erica?

I told you before it's very important

to look after these kind of details

but he really is pushing it too far

with this kind of attitude.

Do we really look like criminals?'

A number of sycophants sympathise kindly.

Normality returns
and with it the ticket inspector.
The man, generous and wealthy,
pays the full single fare.
Peak Period.

It is awkward between him and the woman opposite him.

An unusually long time before we reach Euston
she gets up with her bag and moves down the carriage,
away from the magistrate and his personal assistant.

So a curse on your magistrate's courts
with your all-boys secret society
and your twisted notions of propriety
how many times have you refused clemency?
Mitigating circumstances
are by no means reserved for the wealthy.
Look how you behave when you're standing out in company.

Don't think you can use democracy
like the whore she was never meant to be,
with no humility of equality,
no feel for solidarity,
no notion of mutuality.
And a curse on the spineless who accept this shit so meekly,
power to the woman who shifted in her seat so awkwardly
and spoke her mind straightforwardly.

Leaving my seat, I get up to find her.
She has moved several carriages further up the train.
'Well done for what you said,' I say.
She is nervous, unsure, thinks she's been rude.
'No seriously, you did the right thing,' I tell her.
'Thanks,' she says, 'I feel better about what I said now.'
'My pleasure,' I say, 'you deserve to.'

if you suspect it, report it

Brighton Railway Station; Network Rail

'Excuse me, mate!

There's something I've witnessed at your train station

that makes me a little suspicious.

It's just that the trains never seem to run properly on the

weekends,

and I was just mentioning it because

I've got a sore coccyx from all those

rail-replacement bus service seats I've had to sit on.

And I was just wondering if it's because

there's a *conspiracy*

to stop me having fun on the weekends,

and is this massive hike in ticket price

meant to stop poor people doing anything nice

more than twice a year?

Because I've got this nagging fear

that there's a growing class of people

who can only get to destinations served by the Megabus,

and I don't wish to cause a fuss,

but do I have to listen to these suspicious messages

about suspicious baggages

because the train companies are compliantly

helping the government construct

a divisive climate of fear and mistrust

among the populace?'

If you suspect it, report it.

hitchhiking characters

Thumbing through memiores

I. Somerset

He'd just ticked off Watford to complete the set.
Ticket stubs to all the grounds in the top two leagues
and a growing pile of Stella cans
swilling and clattering in the back.
Another in his hand.
He was pissed.
'Aren't you worried about the police?'
'There's only one traffic policeman round here,' he said,
'and I seen him in the pub ten mile back.'

II. Northamptonshire.

He was an undertaker
with a particular specialism
in cutting down and laying out
suicide victims,
often too dead (or too alive looking)
for the police to want to deal with them.
He said it was true what they say about hanging;
that they shit and cum as the cord snaps them.
'What made you want to do that job?' I asked him.
He paused,
he shifted gear and seemed to think about the question.
'I suppose it was something I always wanted to do,'
he told me.

III. Gloucestershire

His house was on the hill above the church
in the Forest of Dean.
You can't fucking miss it.
Come round any time.

He'd seen a documentary
about salt miners near Timbuktu
hacking away with pickaxes
in the Saharan sun.
Someone should give them a fucking chainsaw,
give them Africans a break.

His daughter was on the heroin.
Once you're on that, you never get off it.

He'd got a fucking motorbike though.

IV. The M25, clockwise

Driving at 60 in the middle lane,

they passed around a joint.

Above us flashed a sign which the driver

read out slowly.

'Don't hog the middle lane.'

Fuck that.

The phone rang.

Yeah we've picked up this hitchhiker.

Pause.

We're going to kill him before he gets off.

Laughter.

Someone was getting married

to someone else's sister.

There was going to be a stag party.

There was a joke about murder.

V. Sheffield

Them fucking Pakis
parking their vans
on the fucking street
to unload their fucking meat.
It's bringing down the country.
It was kind of him to give me a lift though.
Er...
'So you lived in France then. Why did you leave?'
'The 80 year old man who owned the villa
shagged my youngest son.'
We drove the rest of the way in silence.

VI. A9/M9 junction, 25 miles from Glasgow

The Socio-political-economic argument against hitchhiking as
articulated by three men in a van:

'Gerra fookin' motor!'

carriage talk

(Hackney Central - Camden Town; London Overground)

Mm mm gi gi

ka cha cha

O ye menda o soshi ya

I've got to go now

Oh hello

No, I really want to do my best

and commit absolutely to the project

but I don't know if I have the er

time for it you know what I mean?

gi gi

kuka ch ch ch

kala dooba shaba yala

No no, twenty minute... ten minute walk

hm ikra bhavadla archa.

Immy's just finished her thesis
and I've been working all week.
Ha ha.

The next station, mind the platform

aKERCH.

der der der di di der de der
Gi, anti phone na. Ja.
Very frustrating.
dee dee dee dee dee dee de de dee

Eh. Keemey loola?

money into something feel like
away for a few days,
get away.

leaving the protest against the third runway at heathrow

01:00   Two of us leave the protest to get our car and go home.

01:10   We watch from the motorway bridge as cops on the M4 stop a car of young Asian men and put them in the van.

01:12   A team of cops, headed by a middle-aged scouser, stop us for the fourth time that evening, and pat down our trousers again. Canny old man who don't trust us. They search the bridge to see what we've planted there.

Section 1: Suspicion of causing criminal damage.

01:17   The car is pulled over and we're ordered out of the vehicle under section 60 of the Terrorism Act 2000. An angry young man reads our rights under section 1 of the...

'I thought you said it was section 60.'

'I've forgotten, alright? You'd be best to keep your mouth shut, mate.'

I give my name and address and await a FIT team.

'That number plate's been changed, mate.'

'No, it hasn't.'

'It looks like it to me.'

I wrap myself in a blanket and wait.

'You've got no driving licence.'

'As far as I was aware it's not a legal requirement to always carry a driving licence.'

'We'll see what the transport team thinks about it.'

The FIT team arrives and takes our photo for the second time that evening.

'We'll have to get a vehicle maintenance team to check the car's roadworthiness.'

Six people waiting in the cold.

The car arrives. They search it again.

'Our records show no evidence that the car is insured.'
'Yes it is.'
'We'll have to issue you with a ticket for not driving with insurance. If you are insured, you may take your original insurance documents to any police station and have the ticket annulled. In the meantime, your car will be impounded.'

Loaded with bedding and tent we walk the mile and a half back to the campsite through four more stop-and-searches. At one, a policeman agrees to hold our ragged bundle while his colleagues pat down our pockets again searching for the knife we may have picked up in the hundred metres we have walked since the last check-point. His commanding officer is angry with him. He winks at us and keeps holding it.

02:57 'Why are you going back to the campsite now, sir?'
'Our car's been impounded, I thought the hospitality here would be better than at one of your places.'
'John, what reason did I have for stopping them?'
'Put Section 60.'
'Oh, alright then.'

observation

being 20 (For Jan)

Aarhus - Frankfurt (Oder); hitchhiking

We hitched out of Aarhus that summer
to see Firewater play Berlin;
rumbled south with crazy lorry drivers
towards the Danish-German border.
At night we slept on a grass bank
at a service station,
ate bread and cheese,
drank whisky and looked at the night sky;
passed a bottle of a fine single malt
(bought with the thirty pounds my aunt gave me
when she dropped me at Stansted
because she was worried about me sleeping rough);
drank until a mellow peace
glowed warm in our veins and our heads spun,
tongues thickened,
words slurred, outlines blurred,
shapes merged
and we curled up in sleeping bags,

tiny specks under a mass of stars,

the distant roar of the road fading in the darkness.

We drove through Germany with a Polish guy with a thick
moustache,

who called me 'Uncle Sam' and found that funny;

kept checking the effect of his joke:

Me in the back and him with his old, blue eyes

no longer watching the road,

which had taken him, at least half-pissed,

from France where he had got a car cheap.

He dropped us at a junction on the autobahn.

We cowered behind crash barriers

until the police came,

gave us a lift.

In East Berlin,

we stayed in a former squat, now legalised:

A rambling old building, with a flat roof full of weed plants,

walls covered with graffiti.

Christophe, in a black shirt and red tie, Kappa cap,

no front teeth and a neverending bong,

took us around a part of the city,

telling us the ages of all the buildings:

'Dis one vas build in de Second Vorld Var.'

We saw a punk with a perfect red spiked mohican,

posing for a photo by a pillar of the Reichstag.

A thrash metal band warmed up for Firewater,

ended their set naked and rolling in the distortion

and beer-soaked stage,

walked off sheepishly with towels round their waist,

apologised when they smashed a bottle.

The next day,

we were on the road again, heading for Poland.

Me with too many books,

dirty shorts,

cheap trainers,

clothes with holes.

Picked up by the police again,

they dropped us politely at the Polish border.

'Do you have many murders round here?' I asked.

I posed for a photo

outside McDonalds

on Karl Marx Strasse

in Frankfurt-an-der-Oder.

20 years old.

'What do you do?' asked the police in the car,

'I'm a poet-thug,' I told them.

trapped

(West Hampstead - Dalston Kingsland; London Overground)

Sunday morning train
after the party and the three hours' sleep
I carry my bag and my maudlin shame.
Can't be bothered to read,
just watch the falling rain.
I see a drop in in a bigger stream
slide down the window pane.
Everyone ignores the angry scream
of the girl on the floor with the grieving rage.
I get off where a crowd silently seethes,
trapped in the unmanned station by an orange cage.
By the gate, a sign reads:

Emergency Exit. Depress handle and pull lever.

'Has anyone tried opening it?'
I say through gritted teeth.

after we had finshed protesting against the cuts

(Number 38 Bus: Oxford Street - Graham Road / Greenwood Road)

On the bus two strangers argue about the protest

which led us to the park again

just as we had closed down central London

with numbers, banners and chanting.

I join in the debate

on the upper deck of the 38.

'What stop for Richmond Road, mate?'

'Get off here, I'm getting off too.'

'See you later, nice to meet you.'

'There's a party down here, come along.'

He knew his brother. He was going anyway.

It was just round the corner.

DJs spun dub and reggae till the morning.

preacher on the overground

(Stratford - Richmond; London Overground)

On the 07:27 with a ready cry
comes the keening whine of this weedy guy,
who rehearses to the nurses, teachers and builder geezers:

'You do NOT know Jeezus,
you have NOT heard of Jeezus!'

Of course we've heard of Jeezus
he's been dead famous for ages,
you tedious teachers have been feeding us Jeezus
since before our mothers weaned us.
African man, from the black Kings' land
where the kings sold you out and took the religion
of Europeans who claimed that they were God's children:
the people of the light, the light-skinned people,
preaching the gospel truth that all men are not equal.
The Ethiop can't change his skin; it's a gift he has been granted;
one brother owns many others when sugar must be planted.

Now, apparently, at Canonbury we should be thanking God
still
as they did for the high price of cotton stretched
in a Lancastrian mill.

High-buried on a hill, arms slowly sinewing apart
– it seems this image in a dream appealed to Constantine's
heart
and in AD 313, with a cross upon their shield,
Strapped with the arms of the Imperial guards
Christian peace and love took the field.

Now you're telling me of heaven with its pearly gates,
leave me to read Foucault; it's fucking early, mate!
We deserve a break, here our attitudes clash,
all I can hear is:
'Look to your souls; increase your cash;
God will bring prosperity.'
The text of today's sermon is Alan Greenspan…

What do you mean, man? You got it all twist,
you should be turning over tables, not praying to get rich.

Comfort here is twenty Camels and a William Hill sliver,
a heathen sweatshop sews a rich-man's heaven
in the needles' million-eye shimmer,
a few elect cats grow fat and a billion guys wither.
No news under the sun - still the same as ever -
the path is rough and rocky like a road in Caledonia.
From Galileo to Paine, to Malcolm X,
challenge churches from the inside
and you know what's coming next.
Twitchy, ragged preacher man,
with your bag of Greek and Hebrew texts,
Christianity your refuge from a life of lonely stress,
but tell me again, my friend, what are we to gain,
now you have a faith in the after-life
and you're dealing-with-heckler trained?

You say the mandem want to hear,

well, at Camden, let's take a vote.

You go down there and all who want to hear this bloke,

go follow him.

Why did no one come with you, sir?

All men are priests, said Luther,

as he stuck it to the Vatican,

but to stop his monkish head get battered in,

he hid behind a rich man's door that never let the masses in.

New structures were rebuilt; it's not your faith that I dispute,

there's much we'll never know

and I'm not much better off for proof,

yet one certainty is this:

If it's an eternity of bliss

witnessing with you,

then I'd rather take my chances on the journey to the abyss

or Richmond, or wherever it is we're going.

Leave Jeezus alone, leave to rest his bones,

don't talk to me of glory and the grace we'll never own.

For all they've done for the lonely, the mad and the addict,
beautiful painted fairytales aren't the way to break bad habits.
Don't get me wrong, I've always liked the magic:
the poetry of the songs, all that talk of having visions,
the silence clothed in ribbons,
the blessed violence of its rhythms;
but still, it's increasing the division
all this muttering of words
and whose god's got the biggest knob:
it makes the ruckus even worse.
Ladies and gentlemen,
what you have before you is a puppet of the church.
For all that 'love your neighbour' and 'do under others' could
I'll rant as well as thou for mutual aid and brotherhood.

Yet now I leave you with an image of a different kind of man,
who lived up on Clifden Road in a battered transit van
and the text he had up on the dashboard read:
'Ills rain a man'.

lust (on a bendy bus)

After Logue
(Number 3 Bus: Oxford Circus - Crystal Palace)

'Aaah, sweetheart, when's the next one?

I don't know,' she drawls,

red wine flush on tanned cheeks,

'go and have a drink or something,'

the last phoneme ringing in echoes down the phone line.

The bus rocks to a stop and a crone gets on,

breasts long ago sunk too low to show cleavage

in a very low-cut top that does not show it.

Fingers fumble forgetfully over a branded bookshop bag

mouth open in horrified leer,

she groans in loud, vague syllables.

The demented woman on a London bus
Predicts the ruin of all us
The demented woman on a London bus
Predicts the...

Black boys at the back of the bus bang the window

at a chic-looking woman walking past.

Shops idle by and stop,

cheap clothes mean greater spending power.

The boys wear tracksuits, trainers and caps;

two white boys with them,

'Oh my days!'

They swear by that they have not much of,

they talk of blowjobs.

She startles,

crosses her legs as blue light on an early summer's dusk

covers Oxford St crowds shuffling like cards

while manikins stare in their luminous, lewd shop fronts.

She pulls her thoughts together,

her heart beats a little faster,

the crone moans on in her oblivion.

After work with Amanda,
one glass soon became a bottle
and they had laughed a lot
and she told her how she'd met Ben again.
But she didn't tell her how the memory of their kiss
lingered longly on their lips as they danced awkwardly
round each other with words.
But she did say how she'd invited him for dinner
and Amanda had been a bit rude,
but she wouldn't do that, not on a first date,
no, not then,
he'd have to wait.

At the next stop
the boys get off.
They queue by the exit, swaying a little,
like tough wild flowers on rugged tors.
As if she had seen them instead
plunging off the scarp-edge into deep pool waters
the crowds submerge them
and they are swallowed up by another current,
not hers.

Behind her it is lighting up time in Soho.

Blue flames sweep the surface of Sambucas,

change rattles on metal saucers,

doormen survey queues contemptuously;

from open tube mouths

men are released into the night with fire in their belly;

Closed Circuit TV cameras turn their metal snouts.

Later that night,

one of the boys from the bus

will be kicked repeatedly in the head on the floor

because he said she was to him

and he told her that he'd said it

and she told him what she'd heard.

The crone... gets up

and stands by the middle doors expectantly.

Mumbling in low dirge,

clutching her parcel,

she stumbles off into the darkness.

A couple walk past.
Two arms crossed across each other backs
Like the twisted tips of Kitchener's moustache.
And at the point where one bum moves,
a label laps out of the back of the jeans,
like an expectant tongue,
Your country needs you.

Besides the girl, there is only the drunken hum of her thoughts

The doors hiss open,
she hears a man ask about Dulwich
and she glances up,
sees greased, dark hair
greying at the ears.
She thinks of Ben holding her
and she thinks of pulling him,
not just towards her
but kind of into her breasts
and then just as she was thinking of kissing his half-parted lips,
unexpectedly, the man sits down next to her.
He looks straight ahead.

She curses her complacency.

After a pause he asks,

'Do you keep your secrets locked inside?'

A flat, low monotone.

In his briefcase, hardcore nudity,

fist grips its handle, eyes forward.

'My brother's girlfriend is stealing him away from the family.

I must get rid of her.

Shall I strangle the bitch?

Stab her in the breasts and watch the blood flow?'

She knows she will remember

the smell of his aftershave.

'Would you do that?

Would you break up a family

to have a boyfriend for yourself?'

She glances at the gap between his knees and the seat in front.
'What stap you want gal?'
asks a Caribbean voice from the driver's seat.
'Brixton, please,' she says,
gratefully attempting to keep down her panic.

'Do you hold your kisses tight inside your chest?
Do you store them deep inside a treasure chest
and keep the lid tightly shut?
Can I look inside that treasure trove
and take one of your secrets?'

He continues in his monotone
as if repeating the memorised drone
of a church liturgy.
At West Dulwich,
he will get off.

Back in Brixton,
the pushers and the beggars
provide the comfort of familiarity...
she double-locks the doors on her return.

coughing up

(Highbury and Islington - King's Cross; Victoria Line)

On the commuter train
one damp winter's dawn,
quiet save for the distant beats rattling out of headphones
and the rustle of turning freepaper adverts,
a man gets on with a racking cough
and coughs continually for three whole stops.

People strain to look, kiss teeth or mutter,
cover their mouths to shun the germs
of this medieval plague victim,
anachronistically rasping and hacking
his dry windpipe within the well-sealed,
air-conditioned carriage.

Yet, gradually, against their better nature,
throats parch and tickle
healthy strangers start to cough
in sympathetic solidarity.

coughing up

situation

putting some love into it

(Bus number 19a, Liverpool - Kirby; Stagecoach)

Breaths of bus fumes

and shuffling impatience.

'Where do you want to go?' the driver asks angrily.

An old woman stutters and dithers and fumbles.

'Where do you want to go … love?'

he asks again,

this time more nicely.

ode to the bicycle

(around London; Hackney mainly)

To you who dispute its backwardness
know that we ride bikes for a reason;
they take us places we want to go.

Bicycle, we show little respect
for traffic lights. Do not expect us
to wait for the programmed apparatus
to pace through its lollipop functions;
while handbraked engines growl at empty junctions,
we wobble wander onwards towards our goal.

Besides, bicycle,
our internal combustion takes energy too.
Our thighs and calf muscles must consume their carbon,
and energy costs money, remember?
Grant us a few yards before the cars barge past us.

What's more, bicycle,
despite the slanders,
each little gliding cyclist
is one less terrible tonne of metal
in which to thump hard fist on blaring horn
and stamp the brake pedal.
We are not afraid of thudding motorists
we take our own risks and plot our courses

There are obstacles of course.
A cavalry of Clarkson readers mounted on their high horse;
we must weave between them carefully;
and the uniformed infantry
slow of thought and quick to parry pencils threateningly.
They tick the boxes, maintain their force.

And there are traitors on our side too.
Lycra-d arses spoil the view
above my rams horn handlebars, trembling,
ever watchful, they try to steal a march on you
and in a feverish fit of fixie frenzy,
fight to be first in queue
at traffic lights.
Go-getter fitness freaks resembling;
cyclists, you know I'll always defend you, right?
But some pedalists are just posh knobs with a trendy bike.

Think not of them, bicycle, you have your beauty too.
See two fair creatures cuddling at a lamppost
- let me be your hype man, it's my duty to
be your boom, your bap, your bars and toast.
Headphoneless, I rap you tuneless numbers:
downslopes, I freestyle inspiration to take us forward;
uphill, I unpick thoughts that still encumber us -
whereas two cars tangled together
just look a little awkward.

At night, when my mind's in other time,

you take me home in a waking dream,

sweet chariot of mine:

up towpaths, through parks and in an out of little streams

of late cars which fade in glowing taillights.

And should, sibling cyclist, our paths cross in the dark

and you recognise my style,

ring your bell, pass a word, or salute me with a smile.

after

(Brondesbury - Hackney Central; London Overground)

The morning after the train back home
after the post-work drinks in Kilburn
I retrace my steps in the same train seats
without the week-day Metro to distract us
and without the usual faces.

The man with the heavy stupid drunken eyes
and a Costa coffee wake-up;
The woman with the freckled hands
mime-singing to happy music on her iPod,
who is smiling out with saucer eyes at the
brick warehouse estates of Camden;
The shut-eyed woman with a finger on
her sallow cheek and a furrowed pain inside her forehead;
The man in the corner who sprawls his head
and does not want to get to work
this morning.

A pair of rainbow leggings and white platform heels
crossed over somewhere further down the carriage;
A jacket elbow holding an invisible head
that could be a hood bent over trainers;
The fat woman in pink eating surreptitiously
while she reads an article on dieting;
The bald man with *The Times* who could be going on an outing;
The woman with the full, lip-glossed lips
not getting far through her page in the zip-up-covered bible;
And me, with my drunken shame, and without the phone
I left last night in Brondesbury.

borders

crossing the continent

(London St.Pancras - Brussels - Amsterdam)

My mobile phone lets me know I have crossed a border,
radio waves respect the political divisions of land.
Even so, unchanging corporate logos
flash across the continent:
Arriva, G4S and the same named brands.

Multinationals know no boundaries,
place no limits on expansion,
learn every language, cross cultures,
sit at ease in hovels or mansions,
wring money from every colour of hand.

calais

Abdel had lived in France for 4 years – lived in a number of cities – but as he had no papers, he had only worked illegally. Since Christmas 2008, he has had no work at all and now he stays with the other Palestinian men in Calais by the dockside, watching the ferries of P & O and Seafrance go back and forth across the Channel.

That afternoon, dumps of bread, lettuces and other unsold supermarket food were piled up by the dock wall, along which improvised shacks are built: small and dark; flimsy homes for the unmoving migrant. Volunteers arrived from a local charity called Salaam, to give out the food that a nearby Emmaus community had collected.

Further along the same wall were the similar looking shacks of the Muslim-Sudanese neighbourhood. This time, however, Salaam weren't welcomed in peace. Abu came out of his shack, arms flailing angrily, failing to land punches as other men restrained him. The charity volunteers retreated to the safety of the van and drove the hundred yards back to the Palestinian neighbourhood. There Abdel told me that Abu, who had been there for two years, drinks heavily, sometimes bringing his alcohol and bad temper into the Palestinian area, causing some kind of incident nearly every day.

'Life is difficult here,' another Palestinian said, 'every day he causes trouble, but what can you do?'

There is some limited medical provision – official and charitable – for the sick and for the various physical injuries migrants suffer trying to board the lorries that pass through Calais, but there is little that can be done for the mental and spiritual suffering, living as they do, unmoving, unwanted, reliant on hand-outs and charities.

With the Palestinians, however, I was received warmly. A fire was started up and a pot of water placed over the metal cage that acted as a stove. While we talked and waited for coffee, charity-volunteers, political-activists and migrants played dominoes or cards together. Kamal showed me a sketchbook that he had decorated with – in a kind of calligraphic-graffiti style – the names of people whom he had met while staying there.

Abdel, freshly shaved, dived off the harbour wall and swam in the shadow of a disembarking ferry.

***

At the Eritrean squat, we were received with the same generosity of hospitality while they also passed the long day in boredom, waiting for darkness and another chance to smuggle themselves over the sea to England.

A group of Eritreans have squatted a compound of abandoned, boarded up houses and now maybe thirty people live there together, without electricity or running water, but in relative comfort, protected by the compound wall, which the police built to stop them getting in.

Senay thought that five people had got through the night before. He could not know of course what happened to them after that. An activist told us of a recent group of migrants who had made it into the UK and, from their hidden spot at back of the lorry, telephoned friends to tell them that they had made it, whereupon the driver heard them from his cab and called the police. They were arrested and will, presumably, be sent to a detention centre.

Senay was imprisoned in Eritrea as a military deserter (an apparently arbitrary finger somewhere in the offices of the Eritrean army HQ selects certain conscripts to slave on indefinitely after the end of their official 18 months of national service). After a year inside, he and some others managed to break out through a tunnel that they had dug under the walls.

Like 2.5million other migrants, he made his way to Libya where he couldn't find work and was frequently beaten up. He managed to get out and get a passage to Italy, which wasn't much better, and now, finally, he had reached Calais.

With one brother already in the UK, he was confident that he would be able to join him. Tall and thin, softly spoken, with good English, he looked about 25. He asked us about asylum seekers in England. One of our party suggested, aside from the unofficial help of the Eritrean diaspora in England, a number of organisations he can get in touch with, who will try and find him free legal help. She warned him, however, that life is not easy for those seeking asylum in England, and that even someone with as good a case for political asylum as he has (a deserter from the army of a military dictator; an escapee from a martial law prison) might end up in a detention centre. He had been in Calais for three days.

We had come out from London to join the No Borders activists at their campsite as a group of five, four white and one black British. Tewelde, who had been in the squat somewhat longer than Senay, said that No Borders had been "good". In August, much of the aid provision from NGOs in France shuts down for the summer holiday and, during our time there, the most regular visitors (apart from the police) were No Borders and the volunteers from Salaam. Most charities and NGOs have greater resources and infrastructure than Salaam, who, equipped with a van and a squatted base for the volunteers, make regular food drops.

The No Borders activists from UK, Holland, France, Belgium and other parts of Europe come out to join the camp that they had heard about through their own social or political networks to try to establish dialogue, to monitor the police and provide what help they can. The group are non-hierarchical with a changing cast who make decisions and 'policy' in a consensus-based way, coordinating actions or demos, creating and distributing publicity and supporting other independent actions. Naturally, actions, beliefs and attitudes vary with individuals who make up the group at any one time.

The people at the Eritrean squat shared some of their meal with us and gave us some fruit and drinks that had been donated to them.

Tewelde, pointing at one activist, told us that he had come every day for two weeks. He said he had seen many volunteers come and go but, 'this is the first time I have seen a black person', meaning that, until our visit, among the volunteer and activist networks dealing with those paperless people on the French-English border, Tewelde had not seen any black people – an absence that both black and activist communities should reflect upon.

Divided into roughly national groups, the migrants' squatted buildings and improvised camps are spread out around Calais: in deserted buildings such as the Eritrean and Ethiopian neighbourhoods; in woods and fields such as the Iranian and Afghan (both Pashtun and Hazara) camps or along the dockside like the Palestinian and Muslim-Sudanese. While we were there, activists estimated that there were around 900 people in Calais, waiting to leave France. The vast majority are men and, perhaps as many as 700 were from Afghanistan. All the camps are cramped and lack basic amenities.

***

Back with the Palestinians, I ask Abdel if there is anything he hopes for if he manages to make it to England. He left Gaza after his family were killed in Israeli attacks and had given up on work in France.

'I won't get to England,' he replies, 'and if I do, it will be the same as it is here.'

too old to be a guide dog

Dover Priory Railway Station; Network Rail

'Do you think she's too old to be a guide dog? She's fourteen
and a half but she's always learning new stuff; don't listen to
them when they tell you you can't teach an old dog new tricks,
'cause you can, she's always learning new things; she's learned
to wear this coat; she didn't like it at first, she was a bit scared
of it, but now she loves the fucking thing; she's got style, Lucy;
it's falling off a bit but she looks good doesn't she?' asks the
woman on the bench.

'Yes,' politely laughs the nervous young woman next to
her. On this bench in the cold railway station ticket office: two
women, myself and a dog at the older woman's feet. In front
of us people wait, tutting with muttering impatience, to talk
to a person behind a glass screen. Behind us: the Pumpkin
Café and station shop. To our left: the departure screen looms,
hanging over the door to the platform, which is booming and
ringing with monotonous recordings of train announcements.
From the right: noises of boys and BMX tyres and the arrival
of new travellers passing through the station concourse on an

inconstant, higgeldy piggeldy conveyor belt.

A man in steel toe-caps and luminous coat comes in, hurries over to us and, kneeling on his work-jeans knees as if about to screw in a new power socket, starts to stroke the woman's dog. His gaze still fixed on the cross-breed Alsation, he mumbles something and goes into the café-shop.

'Did you hear that?' asks the dog-owner.

'No, I didn't catch it,' I reply.

'Some people say things and just expect you to hear them.'

The man in high-vis jacket returns, mumbling about the price of pop. He hesitates and makes to offer the dog some chicken legs, unwrapped from the tin-foil of what had been his lunch.

'Will she eat this?' he mumbles, head still turned attentively to the coat-wearing dog.

'Yeah, love, she'll eat anything.' Legs crossed, indifferent. The quiet girl with the polite laugh gets up.

'Your train is it, sweetheart?' says the older woman.

'Well, three minutes, I think.'

'OK, ta-ra darling.'

The girl leaves and the woman looks down at the workman - still engrossed in his dog-stroking but now smoking a cigarette.

'Can I have a fag, darling?' she asks.

Blue eyes flash up from their consideration of the canine and fix on the face of her human owner. His hand jerks towards the Pumpkin Café and he says softly, but this time clearly and precisely, 'There's a fag machine in there.'

He reverts his attention back to the dog.

'Do you think she's too old to be a guide dog? She's fourteen and a half but she's always trying new things. Where do you take them to learn that shit? JOHN! You got a tab?'

A man is passing through the ticket office towards the platform, dragging rapidly on a cigarette; he does not hear his name being called.

'JO-OHN!' booms the former mumbling dog-stroker and he snaps his mouth again with a faintly distinguishable crack of teeth. Only momentarily confused, John recognises the woman,

'Alright there, babe,' he says across the ticket hall, composure recovered in an instant.

'You got a tab?'

'I've only got one left but,' pointing to his two-thirds unsmoked cigarette, 'you can have the rest of this if you like.'

'Cheers, darling.'

He comes over, complaining about the price of the café. The dog-owner agrees:

'Bloody rip-off merchant cunts.'

'They've moved the price of the fares up as well,' I say.

'I know,' she exclaims, 'I paid five pounds fucking ten for a ticket to Folkestone.'

John gives her the rest of his cigarette.

Almost simultaneously, the luminous-jacket-wearing, dog-stroking, blue-eyed, chicken-leg-feeding man offers her a lighted cigarette too. She takes them both, places them in her mouth, one between the middle and fore finger of each hand so that they seem to form an equilateral triangle with a corner at her lips. In profile, she is like two Siamese twins, joined at the heads, sharing a cigarette break together contentedly.

in transit

And though each spring doe adde to love new heate,
As Princes doe in times of action get
New taxes, and remit them not in peace,
No winter shall abate the springs encrease.

- John Donne, *'Loves Growth'*.

It astounds me
that, without crossing boundaries,
it's like we had crossed those boundaries anyway.
And maybe I imagine too much, like most bards,
but without visas or postcards,
it's like we were in the Congo,
and you're the only English speaker I know.

I am greedy for you.
We should be ripping into each other
like Shell prospecting for oil in Nigeria,
but I somehow can't make this clear to you
and find myself stammering,
like Moazzem Begg clamouring for release
to the Pakistani police.

We are untravelled travellers,

waiting in transit.

Call my flight number,

tell me to board,

this is one ticket that will afford you

honesty,

and not cost you your

dignity;

you are now entering

security,

and you'll find that I clear all accustomed checks.

for your beauty,

words fail me.

Your lips could silence Rev. Paisley.

You shake your hips,

like Rosa Luxemburg shaking her fist,

imploring me to rise up,

you're a dawn in the distance keeping my eyes up.

For you, I'd die those thousand deaths
as long as we didn't have to die
so that, alive, we could lie
in the soft movement of each other's breath
sleep like there was nothing to wake for,
aake like there was nothing to sleep for,
you are gabba, hip-hop and breakcore,
you are Nana Maroon, Emiline Pankhurst,
when my revolution comes I'll know whom to thank first.

for too long, my eye has wandered,
and I have squandered what I have plundered,
my mind's been left behind with Trotsky's ice-pick through it,
brain-dead, and barely knew it.

But now, there are paths we can mutually navigate,
and beautifully abdicate from the throne of selfhood,

now, let us emigrate to the egalitarian republic of

attainable giving,

now, let us dig and sow a sustainable living,

if they refuse us entry:

let's kick their heads in.

Influx Press is an independent publisher that specialises in
short run, responsive fiction.

We aim to publish challenging, controversial and alternative work that
is written in order to dissect and analyse our immediate surroundings
and produce site specific fiction and poetry.

Please visit www.influxpress.com for more information, books, author
interviews, video content and regular updates.

acknowledgments

This book is dedicated to all those who have brought out what is good in me; who have helped the illusions drop away, held a mirror to my vampiric self-delusion and hopeless conceit; and helped me to see myself better.

It is in thanks to oak trees and cheap caffs; rolling hills, stormy seas and dark pubs; *Ulysses*, street protests and poetry classes; sports games, high grade and kids' laughter; holidays to Wales and roof-racks; *Ode to the Dodo*, *Brand New Second Hand* and *Return of the Boom Bap*.

It comes with apologies for my own deficiencies; with thanks to the too-many-to-mention, to the brilliance of myriad presents that illuminate the possibilities of the future; and with shame for my inadequacies.

In particular, thanks to Kit (the idea originator and a helping hand with the editing shit) and Gary at *Influx* for having faith in me and to Steve at Hammer & Tongue to showing me the way we could go with poetry.

To poets like Dizraeli, Jean 'Binta' Breeze, Jonny Fluffypunk, Kate Tempest, Mark Gwynne Jones and Salena Godden;

To – in order of appearance – Jacob, Simmon, Ross, Andre, Dani, Jonjon, Jules, Andrea, Chris, the signatures of all things I am here to read;

and as much as, if not more than, ever to Maria.

the author

Surname/Nom
BERKSON
Given names/Prenoms
SAMUEL DAVID
Nationality/Nationalite
BRITISH CITIZEN
Date of birth/Date de naissance
09 JUN /JUIN 82
Sex/Sexe   Place of birth/Lieu de naissance
M   FARNBOROUGH

Raised in the London commuter belt towards the end of Margaret Thatcher's first term as Prime Minister, Sam Berkson nevertheless took an English degree at Oxford University. He tried to make amends by working for seven years in secondary schools in Brighton, Liverpool and London.

His first ever poem was a punk piece of visceral disrespect composed upon hearing of the death of Linda McCartney and his first proper gig ended in a fight. Continuing from there he has been performing in UK and abroad regularly since 2002, often under the moniker of 'Angry Sam'.

He has featured at festivals including Latitude, Hay-on-Wye and Bestival, been a visiting poet at KaosPilots international school, Denmark; Grant MacEwan University, Canada; and at the Landmine Victims' Centre, Algeria.

He hosts live slam nights for Hammer & Tongue and the Re: Versed show on NTS radio.

Now resident in Hackney, a poem about his area was part of Influx Press's first publication, 'Acquired for Development By'. He failed his driving theory test in 1999.

the illustrator

Surname/Nom
SOMMERVILLE
Given names/Prenoms
IAIN
Nationality/Nationalite
BRITISH CITIZEN
Date of birth/Date de naissance
01 FEB /FEV 86
Sex/Sexe   Place of birth/Lieu de naissance
M   DUNDEE

praise for life in transit

'What's left of public space after thirty years of neoliberalism? Sam Berkson's new collection, Life In Transit, finds the degraded relics of public space on public transport. Like the music of Burial or Laura Oldfield Ford's Savage Messiah zines, Life In Transit is attuned to the peculiar loneliness of life in neoliberal Britain. In the UK, trains and buses are now 'public' in name only, since most are operated by private companies. By turns lyrical, acerbic and bitingly humorous, Berkson's poems describe a world in which, ordinarily, the only "sympathetic solidarity" is that of commuters who reluctantly cough together. Yet public transport remains a space where our lives can still be transformed by unexpected encounters with others, and where the shadow of another world – collective, egalitarian, democratic - can sometimes be glimpsed.'

- Mark Fisher

'I felt a humane nihilism in these writings: not a usual combination and I found the transport theme very pleasing.'

- John Hegley

'I have always found Sam's dedication to poetry inspiring. He is a poet who cares about language and how it is used. He has the rare gift of being informed and intelligent without being condescending. His poetry delivers his opinions, but in a way that seems to care about yours. His poetry is warm and honest and well crafted. He is a good poet, a poet in the true sense of the word.'

- Kate Tempest